DATE DUE

Metro Litho
Oak Forest, IL 60452

SEP 2 5 1997			

2800-1

338.1 Swallow, Su
SWA   Food for the world

Facing the Future
FOOD FOR THE WORLD

Facing the Future
FOOD FOR THE WORLD

Su Swallow

STECK-VAUGHN
LIBRARY
A Division of Steck-Vaughn Company
Austin, Texas

Published 1991 by Steck-Vaughn Co., Austin, Texas

Library of Congress Cataloging-in-Publication Data

Swallow, Su.
    Food for the world / Su Swallow.
        p.   cm. — (Facing the future)
    Includes index.
    Summary: Examines ways in which the world is experimenting to
produce enough food for its growing population, including farming
the sea, new agricultural methods, and new ways of keeping food
fresh
    ISBN 0-8114-2800-1
    1. Agriculture—Juvenile literature.   2. Food supply—Juvenile
literature.   3. Food—Juvenile literature.   [1. Food supply.
2. Agriculture.]   I. Title.   II. Series.
S519.S895   1991   90-44954
338.1'9—dc20   CIP AC

Printed in Hong Kong
Bound in the United States
1 2 3 4 5 6 7 8 9 0 HK 95 94 93 92 91

Acknowledgments

Maps and diagrams – Jillian Luff of Bitmap Graphics
Illustrations – Outline Illustration, Derby – Andrew Calvert,
Andrew Cook, Andrew Staples
Design – Neil Sayer
Editor – Jean Coppendale

For their help and for information given the author and publishers wish
to thank the following:

Agricultural and Food Research Council (Institute of Food Research,
Institute of Plant Science Research and AFRC Institute of Engineering
Research); Oxfam Overseas Relief and Development Organization; The
London Food Commission; Population Concern; The Association of
Agriculture; ICI Seeds and ICI Agrochemicals; Protan, Norway; Institute
of Oceanographic Sciences; InCA; FARM Africa; Intermediate
Technology; UN Food and Agriculture Organization; Hamish Wilson; Guy
and Teresa Sturtivant; David Field, Royal Botanic Gardens, Kew.

For permission to reproduce copyright material the author and publishers
gratefully acknowledge the following:

Page 19 – ENDA TIERS MONDE, Dakar; page 25 – from a diagram in
New Scientist, London (1989); page 29 – (top) AFRC Institute of
Engineering Research; page 33 – from an illustration by Gary Cook from
The Sunday Times, July 16, 1989, © Times Newspapers Ltd. 1989; page
34 – from an illustration by David Hart from, The Times, February 28,
1989, © Times Newspapers Ltd, 1989.

Cover photograph – *Many plants are expected to be raised by means
of hydroponics in the future* – Terrence Moore, Susan Griggs Photo
Agency

Title page – *Woman winnowing for seeds, Somalia* – Hamish Wilson.

Page 6 – (top) Mark Edwards, Still Pictures – (bottom) Jeremy Hartley,
Intermediate Technology; page 7 – (top) Mark Edwards, Still Pictures –
(bottom) Norman Myers, Bruce Coleman Limited; page 8 – Geoff Sayer,
Oxfam; page 9 – Mary Cherry, Holt Studios Ltd; page 10 – (top) Gerald
Cubitt, Bruce Coleman Limited – (bottom) Hamish Wilson; page 11 –
(top) Mark Edwards, Still Pictures – (bottom) Intermediate Technology;
page 12 – Nigel Cattlin, Holt Studios Ltd; page 13 – (top) Chris Prior,
Seaphot Limited: Planet Earth Pictures – (bottom) Philippe Plailly,
Science Photo Library; page 14 – (left) ICI Seeds – (right) Norman Owen
Tomalin, Bruce Coleman Limited; page 15 – Stephen Pern, The
Hutchison Library; page 16 – Hamish Wilson; page 17 – Hamish Wilson;
page 18 – (top) Ashish Chandola, Survival Anglia – (bottom) Lee Lyon,
Survival Anglia; page 19 – (top) Hamish Wilson – (middle) Francisco
Erize, Bruce Coleman Limited; page 20 – (top) Gilbert van Ryckevorsel,
Seaphot Limited: Planet Earth Pictures – (bottom) Michel Roggo, Bruce
Coleman Limited – (inset) Hans Reinhard, Bruce Coleman Limited; page
21 – (left, top right, bottom right) Inigo Everson, Bruce Coleman
Limited; page 23 – (top) Protan, Norway – (bottom) Robert Jureit, Planet
Earth Pictures; page 24 – Nigel Cattlin, Holt Studios Ltd; page 25 – (top
left, top right, middle) Nigel Cattlin, Holt Studios Ltd; page 26 – B.
Brown, Planet Earth Pictures; page 27 – B. Brown, Planet Earth Pictures;
page 28 – (top) Massey-Ferguson – (bottom) AFRC Institute of
Engineering Research; page 29 – (inset and bottom) AFRC Institute of
Engineering Research; page 30 – (top, bottom) Carl Schmidt-Luchs,
Science Photo Library; page 31 – (top, bottom) Prof. David Hall, Science
Photo Library; page 32 – (left) US Dept. of Energy, Science Photo
Library – (right) Agricultural and Food Research Council; page 34 –
(top) ICI Seeds; page 35 – (top) Martini, Bruce Coleman Limited –
(bottom) Nigel Cattlin, Holt Studios Ltd; page 36 – ICI Seeds; page
37 – Peter Casson, Planet Earth Pictures; page 38 – Terrence Moore,
Susan Griggs Picture Agency; page 39 – Hank Morgan, Science Photo
Library; page 40 – Peter Menzel, Wheeler Pictures, Colorific; page
41 – (top left, bottom left, right) Peter Menzel, Wheeler Pictures,
Colorific; page 42 – (left) NASA, T.R.H. Pictures – (top right)
NASA, T.R.H. Pictures – (bottom right) The Telegraph Colour
Library.

Contents

Introduction

Pictures of people starving to death are shown on television and appear in newspapers whenever a country is hit by famine. Money and food are sent to the disaster area and after a few weeks the famine is no longer an item of news. It is easy to forget that day in, day out 750 million people do not have enough to eat. About 35 thousand people die from hunger every day, 90 percent of them from chronic hunger that lasts all their life, and ten percent from a sudden shortage of food.

Most people suffering from **malnutrition** live in developing countries in Africa, Asia, and Latin America, sometimes called the Third World. Developing Third World countries are poor countries that do not have money to invest in industry. In the rich, developed countries of the world industry has created wealth, and the governments can invest in food production. Three-quarters of the people who live in developing countries live in rural areas and have to grow their own food, with little or no help from their governments. Very often, the soil is poor and crops do not grow well, and the farmers have no money to buy fertilizers to enrich the soil. Harvests may be ruined by drought or flood, pests or war. If this happens, the farmers are too poor to buy food from elsewhere to feed their families.

Poverty, lack of resources, and harsh climates are only part of the complex problem of hunger. The continuous growth of the world population is another key factor. Today's figure of five billion people will probably rise to six billion by the end of the century and may double to ten billion by 2100. Most of these people will be born in countries that are already unable to feed everyone who lives there now. The land is already **overcropped** and **overgrazed**. Water is often scarce. Unless the growth rate is slowed and the population spread out over a wider area, no amount of aid and improved technology will provide enough food for everyone.

Some of the help given to developing countries in the past has failed. This is partly because the large programs and modern farming methods that were introduced needed money and expertise to keep them running,

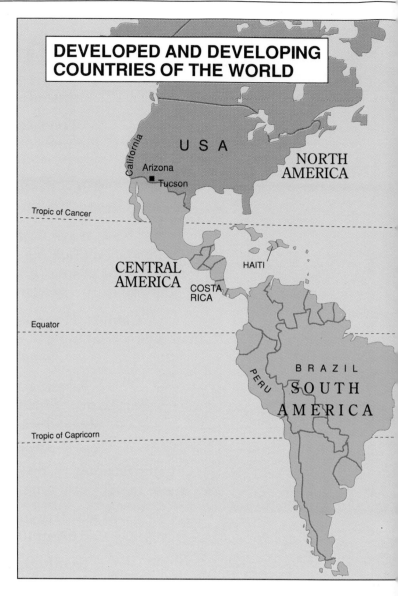

DEVELOPED AND DEVELOPING COUNTRIES OF THE WORLD

money that the local farmers did not have. Aid agencies such as the Oxford Committee on Famine Relief (Oxfam) and the Food and Agriculture Organization (the FAO is a United Nations agency) now organize small projects that help people in a particular area to become more self-sufficient. Such projects have been very successful, and although they do not solve the problem alone, they do hold out some hope for the future.

The first part of this book looks at some of the projects that are helping small communities to produce more food, and which may be used on a wider scale in the future.

The second part of this book looks at some of the ways in which food production may change in developed countries as we move toward the year 2000.

In rich, developed countries most people have plenty to eat, but what is eaten and how it is produced is constantly changing. Farmers

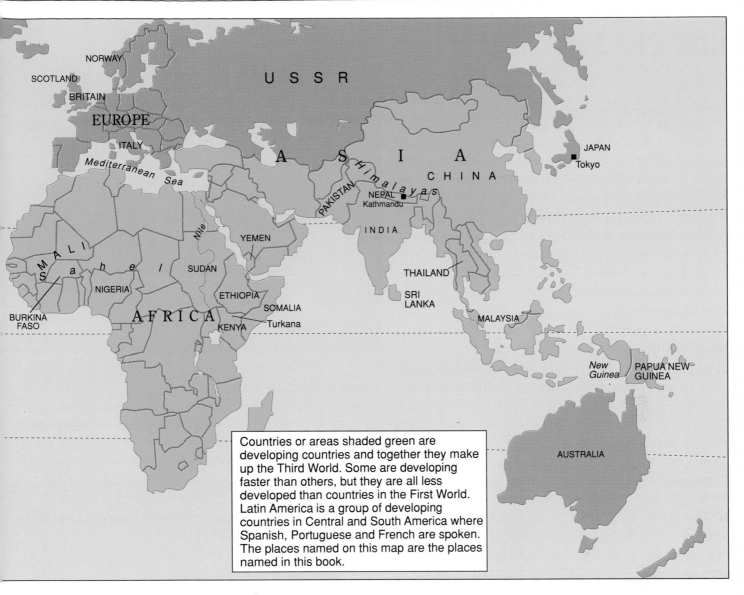

Countries or areas shaded green are developing countries and together they make up the Third World. Some are developing faster than others, but they are all less developed than countries in the First World. Latin America is a group of developing countries in Central and South America where Spanish, Portuguese and French are spoken. The places named on this map are the places named in this book.

may soon be affected by the rising temperatures caused by the greenhouse effect. Some will actually benefit from the change in climate, which will allow them to grow different crops and to farm land that cannot be used at the moment. Others will find that they cannot grow their crops because of the change in climate. Some land may even be flooded and therefore become unusable. High technology will in any case be used more and more to control the environments in which food is produced and processed. Research in Space and under the oceans may provide new food sources. **Biotechnology** is rapidly affecting the way plants and animals are bred.

Public pressure can also affect the way our food is produced. People concerned about animal welfare object strongly to some intensive farming methods. Others are concerned about possible risks to humans from chemical sprays and **irradiation.**

Issues such as these are discussed in *Food for the World*, and you may like to consider what your own views are on the questions set out in the **Food for Thought** boxes. Words in bold type in the text are explained at the end of each section.

malnutrition – a lack of food, especially of the right kind for good health.
overcropped – planted repeatedly with crops so that the soil has no time to recover and loses its fertility.
overgrazed – fed upon repeatedly by animals so that the vegetation is destroyed.
biotechnology – changing living organisms, especially plants and animals, in some way to benefit humans.
irradiation – treating food with radioactive rays to help keep it fresh for longer periods.

Trees for Life

Millions of people in the developing world depend on trees for their survival. Trees provide food, fuel for cooking and heating, and animal fodder. Tree roots trap soil and water, which is important in **semidesert** places. When trees are cut down and soil is left bare, heavy rains wash away the **topsoil,** and the earth beneath forms a hard crust in the harsh sun. The next time it rains, the water runs over the top and away, instead of soaking into the ground. The soil thus becomes too poor to grow trees or crops.

Wood for the fire

Rural people (people who live outside towns) in some developing countries are finding it more and more difficult to grow food, find **fuelwood,** and feed their animals. The forests where they live are being destroyed much faster than they are being replaced. As the trees disappear, and as populations grow, poor people have to spend more and more time searching for fuelwood. In the Himalayas and the African Sahel, for example, women and children spend several hours a day gathering fuel. The more time spent searching, the less time is left for preparing food, a task also done mostly by women. If they cannot find enough wood, they may have to burn animal dung and crop waste, which should be used to fertilize the soil.

Planting trees for the future

Now, some countries have started to plant trees again so that rural people can support themselves in the future. In Kenya, for example, hundreds of small tree nurseries have been set up and half a million schoolchildren have helped to plant trees. In Haiti, farmers planted more than 25 million tree seedlings in only four years. The government of Nepal wants to restore vast areas of forest, and has set up a training center and tree seed store in Katmandu. China hopes to cover 20 percent of its land with forest by the year 2000.

Trees chosen for these projects are often fast-growing species. Some come from parts of the world with similar climates. Others are chosen because their wood burns well, or they can

provide fruit or nuts, and some are grown as animal fodder. The farmers are shown how to take care of the trees so that they grow well. In particular, animals are not allowed to graze among the young trees. Certain trees can be pruned—the branches are cut back every few years—to provide up to ten times the amount of wood that a tree gives when it is left to grow and then felled.

Of course, the trees that are being planted now need time to grow before they can be used. They do not solve the present shortage, but they will help people in the future.

Collecting firewood in Burkina Faso (left). Where wood is scarce, families are forced to eat more and more uncooked or quick-cooking foods, rather than the more nutritious foods—such as beans—which take a long time to cook.

Children in Sri Lanka helping to plant trees.

New forests in China. Like many developing countries, China is planting trees to replace those cut down to clear land for agriculture.

Cooking on an open fire in Nepal (left). Most people in poor countries cook on open fires, which use large amounts of wood. Now new stoves are being made which burn only half as much wood.

Forest farms

One of the best ways to use trees is to grow them together with crops. Some trees take in nitrogen from the air and return it to the soil, which helps other plants to grow. The leaves that fall from the trees also help to enrich the soil. Trees are also more able to survive drought conditions than smaller plants, so even if the field crops fail the farming people still have a source of food and income.

Growing trees and crops together is called **agroforestry.** Some rural people have been using this system for a long time. In Peru, for example, farmers plant corn, rice, cassava, and other crops, and fruit and nut trees. For the first few years they eat and sell the field crops. Then they harvest the fruits and nuts. After 20 years or so, the trees, now past their prime, are cut down. The wood is made into charcoal for cooking and heating. Most families have several fields, each at a different stage in this cycle. Each piece of land in turn is left fallow (uncultivated) for a few years so that the soil can regain its fertility.

Agroforestry is now being introduced in other parts of the developing world to help people produce more food. One recent project in China shows clearly how the system works.

Beans growing under banana trees. Growing crops and trees together can improve the fertility of the soil and reduce erosion.

All in One

The Indian neem is a multi-purpose tree. The seeds can be ground to make an insecticide (which is harmless to people and animals) to protect stored grain from locusts and beetles. The seeds also contain oils that can be used to make medicines and soap. The seed "cake" that is left can be used to enrich the soil. The wide-spreading branches provide shade and firewood. The roots grow deep into the soil and help to prevent **soil erosion.**

Growing neem trees in Mali. These women are protecting young neem trees with sticks to keep the village goats from nibbling the shoots.

Rubber trees on a plantation were planted farther apart than usual, and tea was planted between the rows. The rubber trees grew better because the air could move around them easily, and this stopped the spread of a fungus that had been killing the trees. The tea plants flourished in the gentle shade of the trees. The two crops attracted spiders, which ate the insects, so no insecticide was needed.

Other trees that are mixed with smaller plants include the coconut, which grows very tall and lets in enough light to grow coffee, cocoa, pineapple, banana, cassava, or pasture underneath. This system does not work with trees that cast very heavy shade, where it is better to grow trees and crops side by side. The annual crops can be planted on level ground, and the trees on steep ground where the soil is being eroded. A mixture of trees, shrubs, and field crops provides food, fuel, fodder, building materials, shade, and shelter.

Food for Thought
- How much time does your family spend each day (on average) buying, growing, and preparing food?
- How do you think this might compare with a rural family in a developing country?

semidesert – hot, dry land that has a little more rainfall than the middle part of a desert. Most desert people live in semidesert areas.
topsoil – the fine top layer of soil.
fuelwood – wood that is used for fires for cooking and heating.
agroforestry – the system of growing trees and crops together.
soil erosion – the removal of topsoil, often by wind or rain.

Water in the Desert

Many countries of the world depend on huge **irrigation** systems to water their crops. In India, Pakistan, and China, at least half of the food produced is grown on irrigated land. In the desert areas of northern Africa, only two percent of cropland is irrigated. Low rainfall and drought make it very difficult for people to grow their own food. They have to walk miles each day to fetch water for drinking and for watering plants.

Many organizations are helping desert peoples to make the best use of their limited supply of water. Small, low-cost projects that use local materials and local people are usually the most successful. By copying some of the best ideas used in other areas, more people should have enough water in the future.

Gardens in the sand

Droughts in northern Africa over the last 20 years have forced many **nomadic** families to settle in one place. Many Tuareg families lost their cattle in the droughts and have now settled in villages in Mali, one of the three poorest countries in the world. (See map on page 5.) Relief organizations have helped these people to start a new life by setting up gardening projects. Small wells have been dug at the edge of "maares" (lakes that fill up in the rainy season). Each well irrigates four or more vegetable gardens. Garden tools are made by local people, and families can now grow vegetables such as beans, onions, sweet potatoes, cabbages, and peppers. Similar garden projects are being set up in other countries in Africa.

Magic Moringa Tree

Many people in developing countries take their drinking water from streams and rivers. The water is often muddy and polluted, but programs to clean the water are very expensive. Some village people who live by the Nile River in Sudan have found an answer that is easy and cheap.

Village women collect seeds from the moringa tree, grind them up, and stir them into the river water. Tiny bits of mud and sewage cling to the seed particles, which become heavy and sink, leaving the water cleaner.

Clearing water catchment areas. A farmer in Kenya has made a simple scoop out of scrap metal. The camel drags it through the water in the hollow to scoop out sand and dirt. The silt can be used to bank up the sides of the hollow, so that more water will collect there next time it rains.

Stones stop the water in Burkina Faso.
Lines of stones help to trap rainwater
so that crops can be grown and soil
erosion is checked.

A wind pump in Kenya. A wind pump
is a cheap way to draw water from deep
under the ground.

Magic stones

Lines of "magic stones" have given farmers in northern
Burkina Faso enough water to grow food for their families on
land that is in the African Sahel. (See map on page 5.) In the
past, farmers cleared the stones from their fields and put them
around the edges of their land. Now the stones are used to
hold rainwater and topsoil, so that crops grow better.

First, the men from the village dig out large heavy stones
and break them into smaller ones. Women and children carry
them in baskets to the fields. Then they build solid lines of
stones along the contours of the land, using a cheap and
simple device to find the contours. When it rains, the water
collects behind the stones and sits long enough for it to soak
into the ground, instead of running down the slope and away.
Soil, sand, dead leaves, and seeds also collect behind the stone
barriers, and enrich the soil.

irrigation – watering the land so that plants can grow.
nomadic – belonging to a group that moves its home from
place to place.

11

New Ways with Old Plants

There are about 250,000 kinds of plants in the world, but at the moment we only use about 20 of them as crop plants. One way to help people in developing countries grow more food is to find new plants that can cope with harsh climates and poor soil. Plants that are cultivated in one country are being tried out in other parts of the world. Plants that only grow in the wild today may be cultivated tomorrow.

Plant research can also help in many other ways. Plant breeders can already create crops that resist disease and give high **yields,** by breeding from the strongest plants. They can also produce new varieties of plants by crossbreeding: two plants are crossbred to produce a new plant with all the useful qualities of the other two.

Taking apples to Asia. Apples, pears, and other fruits from temperate areas may be grown on mountain farms like this one in Nepal. The fruits are rich in vitamins and the tree roots help prevent soil erosion.

Genetic engineering

New plants can also be made by **genetic engineering.** A plant has thousands of units of heredity, called **genes,** which determine what the plant looks like, how it grows, and so on. Scientists are now able to pick out individual genes and move them from one plant to another, to improve the quality or yield of a particular food plant. For example, a gene from the Brazil nut was introduced into the haricot bean to make the bean more nourishing. Thanks to genetic engineering, we can now grow strawberries that are not damaged by frost. The world's most important crops—wheat, corn, and rice—have been "designed" to resist disease, to ripen quickly, and to give high yields. The same techniques can improve crops like cassava, sorghum, and millet that are grown in developing countries. For example, seedlings which now die if the ground is too hot could be made to survive.

Plants with a Future?

The winged bean has been called a "supermarket on a stalk." Every part of the plant, except for the stems, can be eaten, and it is rich in protein. It is used in parts of Asia, but it could be grown more widely.

Amaranths, once grown in South America but then replaced by barley, contain a lot of protein, iron, and vitamin C. The grains are used in India, and the leaves in parts of Africa, but amaranths could be grown on a wider scale to help feed people. The buffalo gourd was eaten by the American Indians. Today, it grows wild by the roadside in America, but it could be a very useful crop. It grows well in poor, dry soil, and the fruit seeds contain more protein and edible oil than peanuts and soybeans.

Winged beans in Papua New Guinea.

Varieties of corn produced by genetic engineering. These corn cobs vary in size and color and also in the number of grains they carry.

Protecting wild plants

Plant breeders use modern and old crops to develop new ones, but they also need to use wild varieties. New breeds often have to be replaced after about five years, when they lose their resistance to disease. Yet thousands of wild plants—especially those in tropical jungles—are in danger of becoming extinct as their habitats are destroyed. How can they be preserved to allow plant breeding to continue? One way is to store frozen seeds in gene banks, but it is important to protect plants where they grow. Frozen seeds do not last forever, and some crops, such as coconut and palm oil, cannot be kept like this at all. Also, plants in the wild are always adapting to cope with changes in their environment, and these adaptations could be useful to us in the future.

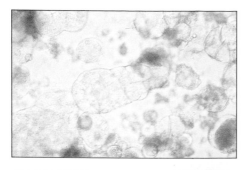

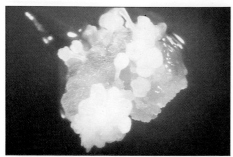

Tissue culture. These are some of the stages in the cloning of a plant. Tiny pieces of plant tissue are moved from one substance to another as they grow, multiply, produce shoots and then roots. When entire young plants have developed they can be planted in soil.

Plants on the production line

Scientists have found another way to produce more food, this time by making many plants from one in a short space of time. **Cloning** plants in this way can be done by a technique called **tissue culture.** In the laboratory, tiny pieces of plant tissue are taken from a leaf or stem and placed in a special jelly. The pieces of plant tissue feed on the nutrients in the jelly and start to grow. Then they start to multiply many times and in a few weeks develop into baby plants. Each new plant will grow to be exactly like the "parent" plant from which the tissue fragments were cut. Hundreds, even thousands, of identical plants can be cloned in this way from a single piece of plant tissue.

Putting in the protein

Some foods that are grown in developing countries are not very nourishing. Cassava, for example, is widely grown in Africa, Asia, and Latin America, but it is a very starchy food with almost no protein. Scientists have discovered that when a special mold is added to dried cassava, a very nourishing food is produced which is high in protein. This discovery may also help countries

Children carrying bread in northern Nigeria.

Bread Without Wheat

Bread made from wheat is very popular in parts of West Africa. The grain has to be imported, which is expensive, but only wheat contains gluten (a mixture of two proteins), which is needed to make the bread rise. Now scientists have developed a new recipe for making bread from any flour, by adding a special kind of gum to the mixture. This means that bakers in Africa can use local crops such as corn, millet, and cassava, and the farmers who grow these crops are better off, too.

that grow bananas. Up to a third of the fruit that is picked is not good enough to export, so it is thrown away. It contains very little protein (about one percent) but some of the fruit is used as animal feed. If the protein can be increased, the banana waste could be made into a useful food for people.

Bananas in a warehouse in Costa Rica (left). Countries in Central America export millions of tons of bananas a year. In the future, the fruit that is not good enough to export could be turned into a high-protein food.

yield – amount of grain, fruit, etc., produced by a plant.
genetic engineering – changing the characteristics of a plant or animal by adding or taking away certain genes.
genes – minute units in living cells which give a plant or animal certain characteristics.
gene bank – place where genes are kept for future use.
cloning – the making of many identical plants or animals from a single organism.
tissue culture – growing plants from bits of plant tissue.

Camels: Hope for the Future?

People have used the camel for thousands of years as a working animal and for food. In different parts of the world it is used for transportation, to pull plows, and to provide milk and meat. Its wool can be used to make cloth, and its hide can be made into shoes and sandals, saddles, and water containers. It lives happily in very harsh climates and survives in droughts when cattle and other animals die. Research scientists have only recently taken a closer look at the camel, but it seems likely that this animal will soon play a much bigger role in helping to feed people who live in the arid and semiarid areas of the world.

Camels can go without water for days. In the dry season, a camel may only be watered every week to ten days, during which time it loses up to a third of its body weight. Then in only a few minutes the camel can take in enough water to last it for another week or so. During this time its body works to conserve the water for as long as possible. It sweats very efficiently and loses little water this way. Instead, it loses a lot of heat through its nostrils. Unlike humans, it does not need to keep its body temperature constant. Rather, the camel's temperature starts very low in the morning and heats up during the day as the sun gets hotter. Nor does the camel lose water in its dung, which is dry enough to burn as fuel. Its kidneys work in a way that prevents any unnecessary loss of water.

Moving in Somalia. This family is on the move in search of water and grazing. The camel is carrying their house and all its contents.

Woman in Turkana, Kenya, milking a camel. It is usually the men who look after the camels but in Turkana it is the women's job.

Camel milk

In some African tribes, the boys who herd the camels live just on camel milk. The milk, which is very white, is rich in vitamin C and high in fat and proteins. This makes it an ideal food, better even than cow's, sheep's, or buffalo's milk, for desert people who have a poor diet. The quality of the milk is not affected by drought conditions, so camel calves can feed normally and people can rely on it when other foods may not survive.

Keeping camels

Camels are also ideal in desert areas because they do less damage than other animals to the very fragile environment. They never overgraze an area: they nibble at a plant and then move on, whereas sheep and goats eat the entire plant. When they walk, their large hoof pads disturb the fine topsoil less than the sharp little hooves of sheep and goats.

Camel-owning tribes have always moved constantly in search of grazing and water. This nomadic way of life will continue to be important if camels are to benefit more people in the future. This is because in many semidesert regions, the plant cover is too thin to support camels in one place all year.

It is also important that camel herders learn the best ways to look after their animals. Experts can give advice on how to obtain more milk from the animals, what they need to eat, how to prevent the spread of disease by separating sick camels, and so on. Veterinary care and better management will also help to reduce the number of calves that die. If such information is passed from one group of camel herders to another, more and more people will benefit from scientific research. As some people already believe, camels may hold the key to the problem of hunger in some parts of the world.

Goats have been described as "wingless locusts." This is because they have very big appetites and, unless they are controlled, will strip trees as high as they can reach.

Preparing to leave the water hole, Ethiopia. Sheep, goats, and camels provide a vital source of food in countries like Ethiopia where it is difficult to grow crops.

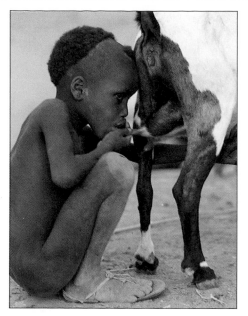

A shepherd boy in Turkana takes a drink from one of his goats. Goat's milk provides children with calcium and vitamins which help to keep them healthy. Goat meat is an important food for many desert people. Goats can be bred quickly and sold to earn money for clothes, rice, and other food items.

A gaur, Malaysia (right). The gaur may be domesticated and bred to provide beef.

Sheep, goats, and gaurs

Sheep and goats can be raised with camels, or separately. By keeping sheep and goats in fenced pens, they can be cared for better, encouraging them to produce more milk. Carefully selected plants can be grown for the animals to feed on, and cut and carried to the pens. This method of feeding prevents overgrazing and damage to the land. The milk, and milk products such as butter, cheese, and yogurt, can be used by the family and surplus food can be sold to bring in some income.

Sheep, goats, and camels have been domesticated for centuries. There may be other animals, living in the wild today, that will be useful to man in the future. In Malaysia, for example, a kind of forest-dwelling cow called a gaur which was becoming extinct is now being bred in captivity. The gaur, which grows quickly and does not need grass (it browses on plants at the forest edge), could soon provide good-quality beef.

Animal Power

Women in developing countries spend hours every day grinding grain into flour, using a pestle and mortar or a hand mill. A motor-driven mill would obviously do the work faster, but it is too expensive for most rural families. Now an animal-powered mill has been developed and it is already in use in parts of Africa. The machine parts can be made locally and the mill can be shared by everyone in the village. Each family uses its own donkey, horse, or ox to work the mill, or the village people buy one animal that is shared by everyone.

Farming the Sea

Fish are an important part of many people's diet in developing and developed countries. More than 92 million tons are caught worldwide, with Japan at the top of the list with 12 million tons a year (the U.S. catches about five million tons and Britain less than one million tons).

As the world population increases, the ocean is an obvious source of extra food. Two-thirds of the world is covered by water, supporting more than 30,000 different species of fish. Yet the main fishing industries take only a few hundred species. It seems very likely that deep-water fish such as giant squid will be fished commercially in the near future. Sometimes people are reluctant to buy a "new" fish. The Arctic pollack, for example, was not popular as a whole fish but when it was cut up into sticks and colored pink to look like crab meat, it sold well. Fish are rich in protein and vitamins but low in animal fats and calories, so they are also a healthy food.

Arctic pollack

Fish farms

Stocks of already popular fish might be increased by adding special food to the water in which they live. A more efficient way is to breed and grow fish in fish farms, a method which has flourished in the last 20 years or so. Salmon, for example, have been farmed very successfully in Scotland, Norway, Oregon,

A salmon farm in Norway. (Inset) Milt, a kind of soft secretion, is being squeezed from a male fish to fertilize eggs taken from a female fish.

Washington, and British Columbia. Hatched in tanks of fresh water, their feed, water temperature, and light are carefully controlled. After a year the little fish are put into cages floating in seawater near the coast. Here they are fed, protected, and treated against disease until they are large enough to be sold. Fish reared in this way can grow twice as quickly as fish in the wild.

Turbot is hatched and reared in a similar way, but it thrives in warm water. In Britain and France sites have been used where the seawater is warmed by nuclear power stations. In northern Spain, the water is naturally warm enough and will be used more in the future.

Scientists are now testing other fish, such as halibut and cod, to see if they can be farmed. Suitable sites near shore are running out, but deep-sea cages are being developed.

Shellfish

Shellfish farming is simpler and cheaper than finfish farming. Mussels can be grown on ropes or in tubes of netting suspended in the water. Oysters can be grown on plastic trays. Lobsters are often reared in a hatchery, then released on the seabed to develop, then caught again.

People in America and Europe are eating more and more shrimp every year, but the wild stock of shrimp is already **overfished.** Thousands of farms in Asia help to supply the market, but feeding the shrimp can be difficult. Collecting or growing **plankton** for the **larvae** to eat is unreliable and expensive. But scientists have recently developed an artificial feed that solves the problem. Tiny particles of a special, complete food are each wrapped in a thin skin which the shrimp can digest, but which prevents the food dissolving in the water.

Collecting krill

The Antarctic may seem a surprising place to find Soviet fishing fleets. What makes such a long and expensive journey worthwhile? The answer is krill. This shellfish looks like a small shrimp, and it gathers in huge shoals in the icy waters around the South Pole, where it feeds on plant plankton. Krill is rich in proteins and vitamins, and could be a valuable source of food for both people and animals in the future. However, there are some problems to solve before other countries are likely to join the Soviet Union, Japan, Norway, and a few others who already fish for krill.

Fishing for krill. When the krill (top right) have been hauled aboard the trawler (left) they are frozen (bottom right).

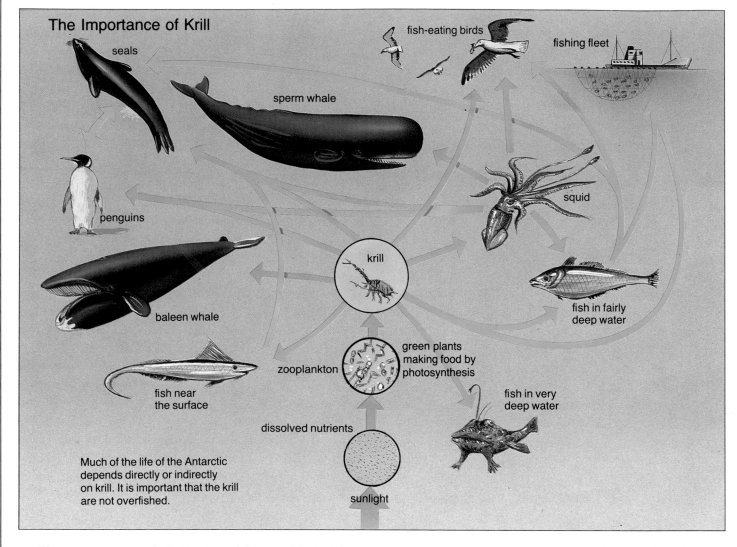

The Importance of Krill

seals

sperm whale

fish-eating birds

fishing fleet

penguins

squid

krill

baleen whale

fish in fairly
deep water

fish near
the surface

zooplankton

green plants
making food by
photosynthesis

fish in very
deep water

dissolved nutrients

Much of the life of the Antarctic
depends directly or indirectly
on krill. It is important that the krill
are not overfished.

sunlight

First, not enough is known about the krill population and its life cycle to work out how much can be fished without affecting the wildlife that depends on these creatures for food. Whales, fish, seals, and penguins would lose a vital part of their diet if krill were overfished.

Even if controls can be set up to protect the krill numbers, there are practical problems to be overcome. The Antarctic seas are frozen for most of the year, so the fishing season lasts for only a few weeks in the summer. Once the krill is caught, it must be processed on board the trawler within a few hours to keep it from spoiling. The shell also has to be removed very quickly because the fluoride it contains would otherwise contaminate the flesh of the krill.

Despite the problems, krill has already been used whole and processed to make a protein paste, fish sticks, chopped krill sausages, and feed for fish farms. Chemicals have been extracted that could have medical and industrial uses. If better harvesting and processing methods are developed, and if other food sources fail, krill fishing may become an important industry in the future.

Vegetables from the sea

The Japanese use seaweed in their cooking. Brown and red seaweeds are harvested from the sea and from seaweed farms. They are often dried and sold in flat sheets or shredded into strips or powdered. They are added to soups and sauces and served as a vegetable stuffed with meat, rice, or shrimp.

A seaweed extract called alginate is widely used to thicken and bind foods together. It is added to all kinds of food products such as ice cream, onion rings, and fruit drinks!

Some people believe that seaweeds will have to be exploited more in the future to help meet the demand for food from a growing world population. Seaweeds have only a limited nutritional value, but there is such a rich supply, available worldwide, and it grows so easily, that research into possible uses continues.

Trawler collecting brown seaweed off the west coast of Norway. Alginate is extracted from the seaweed and used in foods, fabric dyes, and medical products.

Seaweed farm in Japan (right). The large brown fronds are laid out in the sun to dry before being processed.

overfished – taken from the sea in such large quantities that the stock cannot replace itself.
plankton – minute plants and animals that float and drift in the oceans.
larvae – the young stage of an animal that is very different from the adult stage.

More Food or Less?

Since World War II new farming methods and new machinery have enabled farmers in the developed world to mass-produce food. Many countries can produce most of the grain and meat they need. Chemical pesticides and fertilizers, special animal feeds, and drugs help to maintain the quantity and quality of the food; shoppers now expect to find the same items available, looking and tasting the same, each time they visit the supermarket. Even seasonal changes in fresh foods are disappearing. Fruits and vegetables that are not in season can be imported to fill the gap. In some cases, new crop varieties have been developed that can be harvested throughout the year. Research shows that animal breeding seasons can be extended so that fresh lamb could always be available

Some modern farming practices are criticized by people who think our health may be at risk. For example, chemical sprays used to kill insects can stay in vegetables and drain into water supplies. Public pressure has already persuaded farmers to look at more efficient spraying techniques that use less pesticide. The countryside also suffers from some aspects of farming: hedgerows (in Europe) and ponds have disappeared to create bigger fields, insects that are not a threat to crops are killed by sprays, and water plants and animals are affected when farm waste pollutes waterways. Many people are also concerned about factory farming, in which pigs and poultry are reared indoors in spaces that do not allow the animals to move around and behave naturally.

Organic farming

Concern for the environment and for animal welfare, as well as a desire to produce healthy foods without artificial aids, has led to a renewed interest in organic farming. An organic farmer uses traditional, natural methods to produce fruit, vegetables, and meat. He uses compost and animal manure to fertilize crops, he rotates and mixes crops to control pests and weeds, and he allows animals to feed and move about freely. Organic farms need more manpower to produce less food than intensive farms. Some consumers can afford organic produce, but for most people it is very expensive.

Spraying barley with pesticide.

Outdoor pigs (above). Pigs can be kept outdoors where the soil drains well. The arks provide shelter in bad weather.

Sow with piglets (left). When sows farrow (give birth) they may be kept in stalls, in covered yards, or outdoors with small metal or wooden shelters. The stall system prevents the sow crushing the piglets when she lies down, but it restricts her movement.

Although organic farming is growing in popularity, it seems unlikely that it will ever take over from current methods of producing the bulk of our food. The cost of converting a conventional farm to an organic farm is high and it takes several years. Organically grown crops generally have lower yields, although in a few cases, these yields are equal to or better

Laying hens. Hens that are reared to lay eggs are often kept in cages. Four or five birds are kept in each cage and the cages are stacked up in tiers.

ROOM TO MOVE?

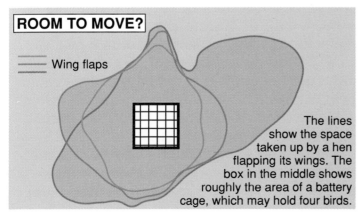

— Wing flaps

The lines show the space taken up by a hen flapping its wings. The box in the middle shows roughly the area of a battery cage, which may hold four birds.

than those of conventional farms. Only one percent of the food eaten in the United States is organically grown. However that one percent may rise to ten by the end of the century.

Chickens: more room to move?

Most egg-laying hens are kept in cages. Heat, light, water, and food are carefully controlled, creating an artificial environment. This is a very efficient way to produce eggs, but not the kindest way. In some European countries, there are rules stating that each bird must have a minimum of 70 sq. in. of floor space in the cage, which it shares with three or four other birds. This amount of space does not give the hen enough room to stretch its wings or to turn around. At present, the United States has no laws regulating the size of the cages.

Outdoor free-range poultry farming is not necessarily the best alternative. The hens suffer in bad weather, it is more difficult for the farmer to keep a check on their health, and they may peck their feathers and attack each other. One answer might be to keep birds in a controlled environment but to give each bird room to move freely. However, any combination of intensive and free-range methods needs more space and more management by the farmer, and so more money from the consumer.

Cows in a modern dairy barn. Should cows' milk yields be increased by giving them extra hormones?

Cows: more milk?

Hormones are chemical substances which control the way a body works. Some are extracted from animals or made up in the laboratory and then used in animal production. Some are used in veterinary care, but others have been injected to make beef cattle grow more quickly. Growth hormones are now banned in some countries, but are still widely used in the United States. Another hormone called bovine somatrotopin (BST) is being considered for use in the United States. If a cow is injected with extra BST it produces up to 20 percent more milk. People have objected to the use of BST because they fear that traces may be left in the milk they drink. They also question whether it is right to force up a cow's milk yield above its normal level.

Breeding: more control?

Until now, animal breeders have used **selection** and **crossbreeding** to produce farm animals with particular qualities (strong, lean, fast-growing, and so on). For example, breeders crossed two breeds of pig (Landrace and Duroc) to produce a variety (called Camborough 12) that will stand up better to life outdoors. But such techniques take years to complete. Now **genetic engineering** can speed up the whole process. Research is still in the early stages, but by moving **genes** from one animal to another scientists will be able to produce animals with all kinds of special features, from fast growth to disease resistance. Biotechnology may also soon allow dairy farmers to control the sex of calves born to their cows. They will then be sure of producing enough milk-producing female cows to maintain their dairy herd. **Cloning** (see also page 15) allows a number of identical animals to be developed from one embryo. This could help in research, but there is concern that some valuable characteristics in a particular animal may be lost in the process.

Nature limits the breeding season of some animals so that the young are born at the best time of year for their survival. Breeding activity

Ewe and lamb. Most lambs are born in the spring, but scientists can extend the breeding season.

in most kinds of sheep is triggered by shorter days in autumn. As the darkness hours increase, so does the level of a particular hormone in the animal's blood. The breeding season can be "moved" by giving doses of this hormone so that, for example, sheep can produce lambs all year, not just in spring.

For or against?

While many scientific advances are clearly beneficial to farming, some recent developments in biotechnology, together with the use of chemicals, drugs, and other intensive methods, cause much argument. The technology even exists to "grow" meat without actually breeding a live animal. Should we support this sort of development? Research will continue, but public awareness can play an important role in guiding that research and in controlling the use to which it is put.

Food for Thought
- Should we change the genetic makeup of animals reared for food? What could be the dangers?
- Is intensive animal farming necessary?
- Do you think people in developing countries would give the same answers?

selection – breeding new plants or animals by choosing parent plants or animals with certain qualities.
crossbreeding – producing new plants or animals by mixing two breeds.
genetic engineering – changing the characteristics of a plant or animal by adding or taking away certain genes.
genes – minute units in living cells which give a plant or animal certain characteristics.
cloning – making many identical plants or animals from a single organism.

Machinery on the Move

When tractor power replaced animal power on the farm, the job of growing crops became much quicker and easier. The tractor is still the single most important machine on a farm, and as its design is improved its ability to work quickly and efficiently increases. Today's tractors are bigger and more powerful. They can be fitted with two or three machines instead of just one. This means that the farmer only has to cover the field once instead of two or three times to cultivate the soil and sow the seed. This saves working time and therefore money. Some tractors are fitted with rubber tracks to spread the weight of the tractor and prevent the soil from becoming compacted (squashed down). This means that crop-growing space is not lost in the tractor's path. Very big, soft "balloon" tires can also be used on bare soil, but they are too wide to use on crops.

It is hard to imagine the tractor ever being replaced, but an experimental gantry or platform, shown in the picture on page 29, could become a common sight on vegetable growers' land. The gantry spans 10 to 69 ft., needs far less power than a tractor to drive it, and can be used for all kinds of jobs, from planting and harvesting to spraying. The gantry has been developed in many countries from Australia to Israel. The wide span between the wheels means that crop and soil damage is kept to a minimum. It is also more stable than a tractor-towed machine, so fertilizers and chemicals can be applied more accurately.

Computer control

A tractor driven by remote control—without a driver—is certainly possible, but it is more likely that computers will be used more and more to help the farmer rather than literally taking over the driver's seat. Computers are already being used to release just the right amount of seed or spray, or to change the speed of harvesting. A tractor of the future, fitted with a video camera and programmed with information from aerial photographs and even satellite pictures, would be able to make detailed adjustments to suit conditions in different parts of the field. Each operation would be recorded on a main computer.

Tractors of the future (above)? A tractor in the year 2000 might have a video display unit and printer, a computer-controlled engine, a remote TV camera, rubber tracks to reduce soil compaction, and an air-conditioned cab.

Tractors for the rice fields. Engineers in Britain are testing the grip of different tractor wheels in a mock-up of a flooded paddy field.

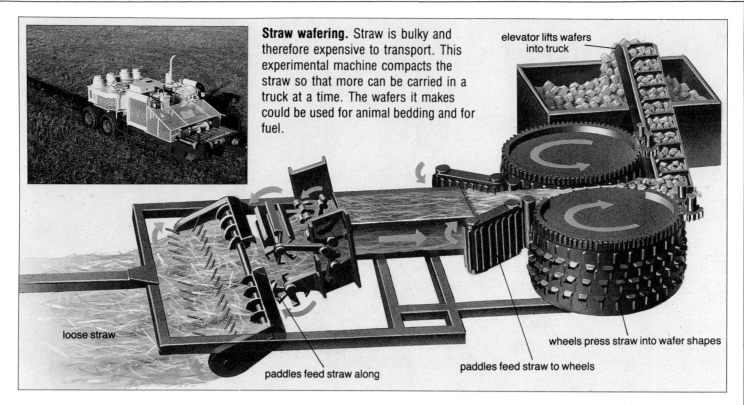

Straw wafering. Straw is bulky and therefore expensive to transport. This experimental machine compacts the straw so that more can be carried in a truck at a time. The wafers it makes could be used for animal bedding and for fuel.

elevator lifts wafers into truck

loose straw

paddles feed straw along

paddles feed straw to wheels

wheels press straw into wafer shapes

Sucking insects off strawberries. An American strawberry grower has invented a giant vacuum cleaner to suck pests off strawberry plants. He no longer has to spray the fruit with pesticides.

Multipurpose gantry (below). The gantry can be adapted for planting, spraying, and harvesting. It can be used in cereal and vegetable crops and can be up to 69 feet wide.

Synthetic Foods

When is a potpie not a potpie? Answer: when it is a textured vegetable protein (TVP) pie. Since the 1950s it has been possible to make all kinds of meat products, such as chopped meat, sausages, and stews, without using meat. Soybeans are used instead. First the oil (which can be used to make margarine) is removed. Then the beans are ground to make a flour. The flour is then treated in different ways to give it the flavor and texture of meat, and formed into strips, chunks, or particles which can be dried for storage.

Soybeans are very rich in protein, they are easy to grow, and are more economic to farm than animals. A field of soybeans provides protein for nearly 30 times more people than the same area grazed by cattle. This plant is already widely grown in America and Asia, and on a limited scale in parts of Africa and Europe. TVP from soybeans could be an important source of nutritious food for people in developing countries, although at the moment it is still too expensive to process.

Soybean harvest in America. The combine harvester (below) fills a container with ripe pods of the soybean plant (above).

Aquaculture

One species of **algae** could be used to make a food that is high in protein. Algae are a group of plants that includes seaweeds, but many single-celled algae live in fresh water. The scum that forms on a stagnant pond is an alga.

Some algae are already grown commercially on big ponds and used to feed fish and farm animals. One alga called *spirulina* is used in health foods. It has so much protein—much more than soybeans, for example—that it may be grown on a bigger scale in the future.

Growing plants in water—known as aquaculture—could be a useful method of producing food where soil is not available (for example, in Space) or where the soil is too poor to support land plants.

Algal ponds in Thailand (top left). Mixed algae are grown in ponds to feed fish and shrimp on farms.

Harvesting algae (bottom left). A blue-green alga, spirulina, is filtered from the water on a simple sieve table.

Fungus foods

We already eat all kinds of fungi, from mushrooms to blue mold in cheese. A new food, called mycoprotein, is made from a tiny fungus that is too small to see without a microscope. Food scientists tested 3,000 soil samples from all over the world to find a suitable fungus for making a high-protein food. The fungus is grown in a large vessel called a fermenter, in a sugar solution made from wheat or other cereal waste. Then it is filtered and dried on a conveyor belt. At this stage it is chewy like meat, but pale and fairly tasteless, with a faint smell of mushrooms. Then it is colored and flavored to look and taste like hamburgers, chicken pieces, fish sticks, and many other dishes.

Single-cell protein

Mycoprotein is a single-cell protein (SCP), a protein food made from single-celled organisms. Other SCP foods are already made as animal feeds, and scientists are working to develop them into food for people. The tiny organisms can be grown on fuels such as oil, methane, and gas, as well as on agricultural waste. If SCP foods form a bigger part of our daily diet in the future, then farms could increasingly give way to food factories (see also page 38). In developing countries, SCP foods could help where the harsh climate and poor soil make growing crops difficult.

Food for Thought
- What are the possible benefits of these human-made protein foods to people in the developing and developed world?
- Have you tried any of the products described on these pages? Why do you think they are often made to resemble foods we already eat?

algae – a group of plants that grow in the ocean and in fresh water.

Keeping Food Fresh

In the past, people preserved food by salting, drying, smoking, or pickling. In cold climates, meat and fish could literally be deep-frozen in pits dug in the ice. The same methods are still used today, although the work can now be done by machine. Most food in supermarkets also contains certain **additives** which extend its "shelf-life"—the time it can be kept in good condition for sale. Some additives work by stopping the enzyme (protein substances in the food) breakdown which spoils the food. Others prevent bacteria and molds from growing.

How many additives?

The rules about the use of additives vary from one country to another. In Britain, about 2,000 additives are allowed for sweetening, coloring, flavoring, and preserving foods. Most of them have to be listed in the ingredients on the packaging, which are given in the order of quantity so that the first item is the main ingredient. In the European Economic Community (EEC), an organization of 12 European countries, about 99 of the additives allowed are preservatives. The most common is sulfur dioxide. Most of us eat foods containing sulfur dioxide every day—crackers, fruit juice, sugar, jam, instant mashed potatoes, canned fruit. It keeps food from spoiling and preserves vitamin C.

Some additives are used not to preserve the food but to make the food look attractive. Lemons and oranges are often sprayed with a wax to make the skins look shiny.

Many people feel that the use of additives should be limited to those that are strictly necessary. They are concerned that not enough is known about the long-term effect on our health of eating foods containing additives, even though they appear to be safe. Some countries have banned certain additives that can cause allergies. Norway, for example, has banned the use of all artificial colorings. Even when additives are listed on food labels, as in Britain, not all the information is necessarily given. In the United States, all ingredients must be listed according to concentration, but unwrapped foods, such as bakery-bought items and fast foods are unlabeled.

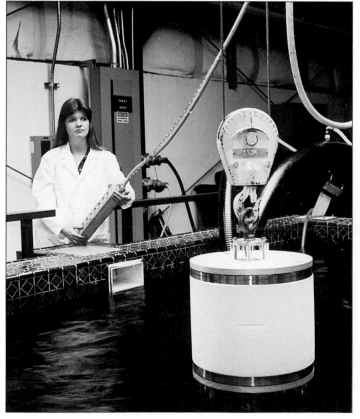

Apples in storage (above). These apples have been stored for four weeks. The apples kept in special packaging (left) have kept better than apples from the control pack.

Laboratory tests in California (left). The drum containing fruit is about to be submerged in the pool, where the food will be irradiated with Xrays.

Wrapped in plastic

Fresh fruit and vegetables have to stay in good condition for at least several days between being picked and being eaten. Plastic wrappers that allow the food to ''breathe'' by allowing gases and water vapor to escape can prevent apples from turning yellow, mold from growing on tomatoes, and can prevent root vegetables from pushing out new roots. Holes punched in bread wrappers prevent the crust from softening by letting the moisture out. New packaging is constantly being developed.

Recipe for irradiation

Irradiation as a method of treating food to keep it fresh and to destroy food-poisoning bacteria has created a big debate in some countries. At the beginning of 1990 Britain was still considering whether to allow its use. The process is allowed on a limited range of foods in more than 30 countries, including the United States, France, and Holland. Other countries such as Australia, West Germany, and Sweden have banned its use. The food is treated with **gamma rays** from radioactive material or with electrons. Irradiated fruit ripens more slowly and stays mold-free longer. Potatoes treated in this way do not sprout while being stored. The risk of food poisoning is lessened—the salmonella bacteria in chicken, for example, is destroyed by the irradiation process. The taste and texture of many foods seem to improve. But irradiation destroys certain vitamins, it is not effective on all foods (for example dairy products and some fruits and meats), and does not kill all organisms that cause disease. The long-term effects of eating irradiated food are still being debated, although scientists have been investigating the process for many years. Nevertheless, many people are concerned about the dangers to health.

Food for Thought
● How would you organize a campaign to stop the use of an additive or a way of treating food which you thought could damage people's health?

---

additives – natural or artificial ingredients that are added to foods.
irradiation – treating (food) with radioactive rays to help keep it fresh.
gamma rays – radiation given off by radioactive substances.

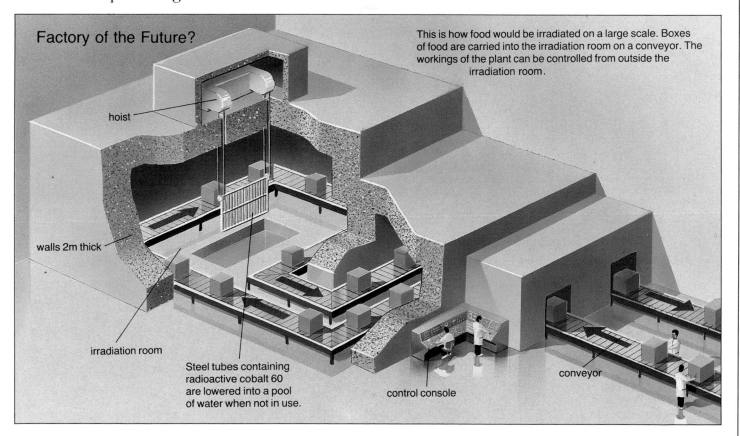

Factory of the Future?

This is how food would be irradiated on a large scale. Boxes of food are carried into the irradiation room on a conveyor. The workings of the plant can be controlled from outside the irradiation room.

hoist

walls 2m thick

irradiation room

Steel tubes containing radioactive cobalt 60 are lowered into a pool of water when not in use.

control console

conveyor

Farms of the Future

The farmer decides what to grow, but he does not really have a free choice. Factors outside his control affect which crops will grow and sell well. In the future, farming will also be affected by the **greenhouse effect**, advances in **biotechnology**, and the need to reduce food surpluses.

Corn in America (above).
Sunflowers in Italy (right). Crops that grow well in warm, dry conditions, such as corn and sunflowers, may be grown farther north as the greenhouse effect changes our climate.

A new climate

Farmers have always had to cope with local changes in the climate, but food producers all over the world will soon be affected by the greenhouse effect. As more and more carbon dioxide (for example, from burning forests and fossil fuels such as coal and oil) pollutes the atmosphere, the world is becoming warmer. No one can forecast exactly what the temperature will be, but experts predict that temperatures in the northern hemisphere could rise by between 5°F to 14°F over the next 50 years. Even very small changes in temperature could be disastrous to populations in some parts of the world. For example, semiarid areas would become even more threatened by drought. Rice could not be grown in a drier climate. Large areas of coastal land could be flooded as the ice caps melted.

It is obviously important to limit the greenhouse effect, but some scientists are already considering ways in which farming

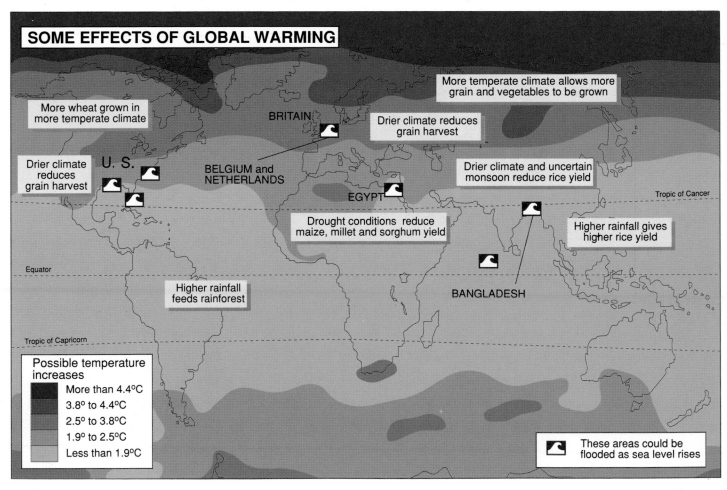

SOME EFFECTS OF GLOBAL WARMING

More temperate climate allows more grain and vegetables to be grown

More wheat grown in more temperate climate

BRITAIN

Drier climate reduces grain harvest

Drier climate reduces grain harvest

U. S.

BELGIUM and NETHERLANDS

Drier climate and uncertain monsoon reduce rice yield

Tropic of Cancer

EGYPT

Drought conditions reduce maize, millet and sorghum yield

Higher rainfall gives higher rice yield

Equator

Higher rainfall feeds rainforest

BANGLADESH

Tropic of Capricorn

Possible temperature increases
- More than 4.4°C
- 3.8° to 4.4°C
- 2.5° to 3.8°C
- 1.9° to 2.5°C
- Less than 1.9°C

These areas could be flooded as sea level rises

could be adapted to cope with the possible changes in climate. Some farmers in certain northern countries could actually benefit from a global warming. Warmer, wetter weather would allow them to grow cereals, fruits, and vegetables that cannot survive there at present. It could also give them higher yields of existing crops. In Britain, for example, farmers may be able to grow sun-loving crops such as soybeans, sunflowers, and grapes. They may even export them to countries that will no longer be able to grow them.

Other changes will also take place. As the temperature rises and the pattern of rainfall changes, the farming calendar will change. Different jobs will be done earlier or later in the year than now to take advantage of the longer growing season. Varieties of crops will change, too, to suit the new weather.

Cereals being tested. The test field is divided into small plots and each one is sown with a different variety of wheat. The crops are checked for growth rate, disease resistance, and yield.

Looking for an alternative

During most years in the United States, more food is produced than can be used by its citizens. Some of this extra, or surplus, food is stored for up to a year in case poor weather causes reduced crops later on. About one-third of the food is sent to other countries. The United States exports more farm products than any other country in the world.

The United States government must limit how much farmers produce, in order to prevent wasteful surpluses and to keep prices of farm products from dropping too low. In 1990, the government paid farmers $10 billion to reduce farm production. In exchange for government payments, some farmers agreed to take about 40 million acres of farmland out of production for the next ten years.

However, the government is finding it necessary to cut spending, and Congress is proposing to reduce the amount of government money paid to farmers. When that happens, farmers who produce large surpluses will have to accept lower prices or find other ways to make money. Some farmers may practice **organic farming** (see page 25). They can get three to four times as much money for organic produce as for that raised with chemicals or other artificial aids. Some may plant trees for timber products. Other farmers may devote part of their land to recreational purposes (golf courses, parks, bed-and-breakfast inns, fishing resorts, and so forth).

Science takes control

Genetic engineering will allow scientists to develop new varieties of crops for particular jobs: potatoes that are good for chips, wheat that is good for making bread (or crackers or animal feed), and so on. They will be able to "design" crops that are resistant to pests and diseases and that can tolerate different weather conditions. They will be able to alter fruits so that they ripen slowly without going soft. The possible benefits of biotechnology to farming seem endless and will certainly shape the farms of the future.

Chemical sprays, which are expensive and which harm wildlife and water supplies, may be replaced by more natural methods of protection. Researchers have already developed a pesticide from bacteria found in the soil. Crop seeds could be treated with the pesticide, which would then attack and dissolve any fungus or pest insect that attacked the plant. Natural predators may be deliberately introduced to control certain crop pests. This biological method is already used in greenhouses where crops such as tomatoes and cucumbers are grown: a small wasp is introduced to eat the aphids.

An American has invented a very different kind of crop protection. It is a spray that coats fruit trees and vegetables with a thin film of plastic.

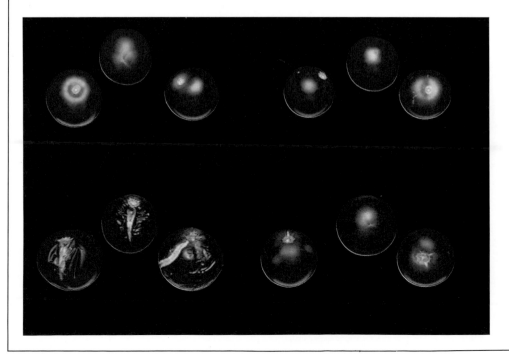

Producing firm tomatoes. Huge quantities of tomatoes spoil before they can be sold. In the picture, the tomatoes on the left are ordinary tomatoes before and after storage. The ones on the right are a new genetically engineered variety that ripen without going soft. They could be for sale by 1993, when tests have been completed.

The plastic coating protects the crops during droughts by reducing the amount of moisture that is lost through leaves and stems. It can also protect against cold and freezing conditions.

Healthy foods

New food crops are tried out as people become more concerned with the effect of diet on health. Many people want more natural ingredients in **processed food** and fewer artificial additives. The American blueberry, for example, would grow well in Britain and could be sold fresh or used for processing. Fruits that grow wild in Britain, such as the sea buckthorn and rosehips, are already used in the Soviet Union and Europe because they are rich in vitamins. Such crops could be grown commercially for making jams, fruit juices, and natural food colorings.

As meat substitutes become more popular, other crops such as soybeans may be grown more widely where the climate is suitable (see page 30).

Food from the wild. Wild plants such as the sea buckthorn, which grows on sandy coasts in Britain, could be grown as food crops.

Factory-fresh vegetables

As high technology takes over, some farming is moving off the land and into custom-built buildings. In Japan, for example, a factory farm has been built in Tokyo in which lettuces are grown on conveyor belts and delivered direct to the supermarket next door. The plants are grown by a system of **hydroponics,** not in soil but on a special mat. The plants are fed with liquid nutrients and grow from seed several times faster than normal. Computers control the lighting, air conditioning, and temperature. In this artificial environment there is no need for pesticides or herbicides, and the farmer does not worry about the weather.

Growing vegetables in this way uses less space and fewer working hours than traditional methods of cultivation, and it is also more reliable. Hydroponics could be used in many ways in the future. Animal fodder, for instance, could be produced quickly and efficiently. In the U.S., grass for cattle is grown on trays stacked one above the other in tall buildings, and the system has recently been introduced into Britain. The same system may be used to grow crops such as wheat and corn in Space (see page 43). Hydroponic food factories could also be useful in developing countries with low or unreliable rainfall. Plants grown by this method need only one-fifth the amount of water needed by plants grown in the field.

greenhouse effect – the rise in temperature around the world caused by pollution in the atmosphere.
biotechnology – changing living organisms, especially plants and animals, in some way to benefit humans.
organic farming – farming without artificial aids such as pesticides.
processed food – food products that are made in a factory from a number of basic ingredients.
hydroponics – a method of growing plants without soil, using a nutrient solution.

Salad crops (right). Vegetables and salad crops are already grown on a large scale using hydroponics.

Hydroponics (below). Spinach plants are sprayed with liquid food and water as the plastic drum spins around, holding the plants in place.

Under Glass in the Desert

Imagine being shut in a giant greenhouse in the desert for two years, and having to grow all your own food during that time. In your leisure periods you can watch television, go scuba-diving in a mini ocean 26 feet deep, or camp in a small desert area (still under glass, of course), but—unless you become seriously ill—you cannot leave the greenhouse, nor can anyone visit you from the outside! This is what a group of eight research scientists started doing in September 1990, when Biosphere II was sealed up for a two-year experiment. The scientists want to find out more about the ecology of the Earth, and work on systems that could help in setting up stations in Space or on other planets.

Biosphere II (Biosphere I is the Earth) is a glass and steel structure that covers about two and a half acres near Tucson, Arizona. It is designed to imitate life cycles on Earth, in miniature. It contains several tropical habitats: desert, ocean, marsh, savannah (grassland), and rain forest. Each area has a range of plants and animals that copy the balance of life found in the wild.

The Arizona project is a self-contained unit in which air, water, and waste will be continuously recycled. Two underground chambers allow the air to expand as it is heated by the sun. Otherwise the increase in air pressure would cause the glass or the seals to break. Solar power provides electricity. The scientists have their own apartments and are able to communicate with the outside world.

Diseased plants can be replaced using tissue culture.

Pest control. Ladybugs will be used to help control plant pests without pesticides.

Fish will be reared in large tanks (right).

Home-grown food

The research team will grow 150 different food crops. About a third of these will be ready for picking at any one time. Plant pests will be controlled by ladybugs, small wasps, and other insect predators, not by chemical sprays. The soil will be fertilized with waste materials. Diseased plants can be replaced quickly with new stock grown by the tissue culture method (see page 14) in the laboratories in Biosphere II. The scientist-farmers will keep about 30 chickens for eggs and meat, three pygmy goats for milk, and pigs for meat. Fish tanks will provide not only fish, but rice too, grown in the water and fed by nutrients from the waste of an African fish known as the tilapia.

Of course, it is possible that the project will have to be abandoned before the two years are up, because of some disaster inside or outside the sealed greenhouse. But if it is successful, the work of the scientists in Biosphere II could provide new ideas for food production on Earth as well as in Space.

Food for Thought
- What might it be like to live in Biosphere II for two years? What problems might you have to face?
- What kind of person might be chosen to take part in the project?

A model of the Biosphere II buildings (left).

41

Dining in Space

The first men in Space dined on liquid food which they squeezed out of tubes and sucked through a straw. The food had little taste or texture. Since then scientists have found ways to produce Space meals that are more like Earth food. Today, the astronauts who set off on a shuttle mission have their dinner served on a tray, eat with a knife and fork, and have a choice of nearly 100 dishes, from salmon to scrambled eggs.

But dining in Space is not quite like having a TV dinner at home in front of the television. The tray is strapped to the astronaut's leg—or fixed to the wall—to keep it from floating away, and it is shaped to hold various food packages in place, each wrapped separately. Some packages have a lid. Others have to be cut open with scissors. Salt and pepper are in liquid form and drinks—even tea and coffee—are taken through a straw. A clamp keeps the liquid from flowing out of the straw between mouthfuls.

On board the Soviet Soyuz spacecraft. Astronauts used to eat out of tubes, like these tubes labeled ''vodka'' which contained beet soup!

Space food today. Meals in Space are served on a tray.

On board the shuttle (left). Astronauts strap themselves and their food trays down, ready to eat.

So far, there is no refrigerator on board the shuttle so any fresh food (bread, fruit, sticks of carrot and celery) has to be eaten in the first two or three days. The rest of the food is precooked or treated so that it can be stored without a refrigerator. Some of the foods, such as soups, casseroles, and cereals, are freeze-dried: the food is frozen, then heated gently—not enough to melt it but just enough to draw out the water as vapor. Just before the food is eaten, water is added through a hollow needle pushed into the base of the container. Some foods are heated in an oven in the shuttle's galley (kitchen).

When the astronauts have finished their meal, the food containers and any other garbage is collected in plastic sacks and stored in a compartment under the floor until the shuttle returns to Earth. There is no sink for washing up; in Space, water forms droplets which float around, so trays and cutlery are simply wiped clean with a moistened cloth.

Living in Space

If plans for a Space station or even a lunar base become a reality, people will stay in Space for long periods of time. Scientists are looking at different ways of producing fresh food in Space. Peas will be taken on the Juno spaceflight to the Soviet Space station Mir to see how they grow at zero gravity. Other crops such as wheat and corn could be grown in stacked trays in a spacecraft, without soil, using **hydroponics** (see page 38). Algae could be grown using the astronauts' waste water (see page 31). It may even be possible to grow vegetables in the soil on the Moon.

Food for Thought
- Look at the astronauts' menu on this page. Why is it a good diet for a day?
- What food and drink would you take with you on a journey into Space? Plan a day's menu.
- What do you think people will be eating in Space in the next century?

hydroponics – a method of growing plants without soil, using a nutrient solution.

Eating in Orbit

A typical menu for a day aboard the shuttle gives each astronaut a balanced diet, with sufficient vitamins and minerals. Each person's food packages are marked with a different colored dot.

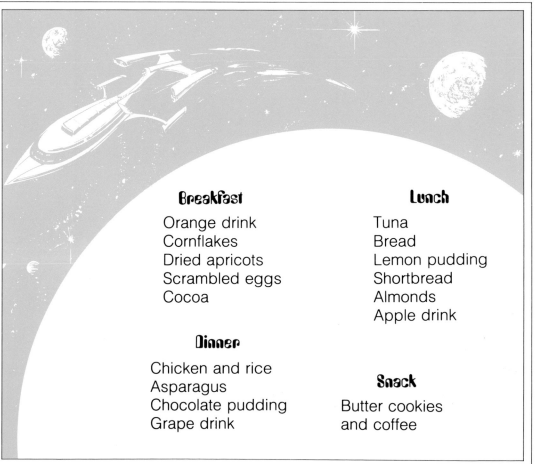

Breakfast

Orange drink
Cornflakes
Dried apricots
Scrambled eggs
Cocoa

Dinner

Chicken and rice
Asparagus
Chocolate pudding
Grape drink

Lunch

Tuna
Bread
Lemon pudding
Shortbread
Almonds
Apple drink

Snack

Butter cookies
and coffee

Conclusions

As the world population rises, the need to produce enough food for everyone becomes more and more urgent. Some of the major causes of hunger—flood, drought, pests (such as locusts), and war—seem to be beyond our control. Yet projects like those described in this book show that it is possible, on a small scale at least, to face the future with some degree of hope. Some of the most successful projects give quite simple, practical help and require little or no outside help once they are established. Advances in science, especially in biotechnology, can also benefit the developing countries in many different ways. If enough help of the right kind is given by the developed countries to the Third World, then perhaps fewer people will die of starvation in the future.

In developed countries, advances in science have meant that we produce more than enough food for our needs. There is a much greater variety of high-quality food available than ever before, but many people are worried about the way in which the food is produced. Modern intensive farming raises questions about our health, the environment, and the well-being of animals. It seems inevitable that most of our food will be produced by fewer and fewer farms, which will be more like factories than fields. Yet as public awareness grows, there is a movement toward producing at least some of our food by more traditional methods. If we can combine the best of technology with the best of tradition, then perhaps we can face the future with optimism.

Glossary

additives – natural or artificial ingredients that are added to foods.

agroforestry – the system of growing trees and crops together.

biotechnology – changing living organisms, especially plants and animals, in some way to benefit humans.

cloning – the making of identical plants or animals from a single organism.

crossbreeding – producing new plants or animals by mixing two breeds.

genes – minute units in living cells which give a plant or animal certain characteristics.

genetic engineering – changing the characteristics of a plant or animal by adding or taking away certain genes.

greenhouse effect – the rise in temperature around the world caused by pollution in the atmosphere.

hydroponics – a method of growing plants without soil, using nutrient solutions.

irradiation – treating food with radioactive rays to help keep it fresh for longer periods.

irrigation – watering the land so that plants can grow.

malnutrition – a lack of food, especially of the right kind for good health.

organic farming – farming without artificial aids such as pesticides.

overcropped – planted repeatedly with crops so that the soil has no time to recover and loses its fertility.

overfished – taken from the sea in such large quantities that the stock cannot replace itself.

overgrazed – fed upon repeatedly by animals so that the vegetation is destroyed.

processed food – food products made in a factory from a number of basic ingredients.

selection – breeding new plants or animals by choosing parent plants or animals with certain qualities.

semidesert – hot, dry land that has a little more rainfall than the middle part of a desert. Most desert people live in semidesert areas.

yield – amount of grain, fruit, etc., produced by a plant.

Further Reading

Famine in Africa Lloyd Timberlake (Watts, 1986)

Farming and the Environment Mark Lambert (Steck-Vaughn, 1990)

The Fishing Industry Nancy W. Ferrell (Watts, 1984)

Food or Famine Christopher Gibb (Rourke, 1987)

Food Plants Jennifer Cochrane (Steck-Vaughn, 1990)

Future World of Agriculture Wendy Murphy (Watts, 1984)

Grasses and Grains Theresa Greenaway (Steck-Vaughn, 1990)

The Hunger Road John C. Fine (Macmillan, 1988)

Rice Sylvia A. Johnson (Lerner, 1985)

The Spread of Deserts Ewan McLeish (Steck-Vaughn, 1990)

Waste and Recycling Barbara James (Steck-Vaughn, 1990)

Index

First published in
England, 1990, by
Evans Brothers Ltd., London